TITLE I
HOLMES JR HIGH
2001-02

# GALAXY OF SUPERSTARS

Ben Affleck

Backstreet Boys

Garth Brooks

Mariah Carey

Cameron Diaz

Leonardo DiCaprio

Tom Hanks

Hanson

Jennifer Love Hewitt

Lauryn Hill

Ewan McGregor

Mike Myers

'N Sync

LeAnn Rimes

Britney Spears

Spice Girls

Jonathan Taylor Thomas

Venus Williams

CHELSEA HOUSE PUBLISHERS

GALAXY OF SUPERSTARS

# Cameron Diaz

## Anne E. Hill

CHELSEA HOUSE PUBLISHERS
*Philadelphia*

Frontis: *Cameron Diaz, whose tremendous talent has ignited the world of movies. Although she has achieved superstardom, Cameron simply continues to be herself while trying to live life to the fullest.*

Produced by
21st Century Publishing and Communications, Inc.
New York, New York
http://www.21cpc.com

CHELSEA HOUSE PUBLISHERS

Editor in Chief: Stephen Reginald
Managing Editor: James D. Gallagher
Production Manager: Pamela Loos
Art Director: Sara Davis
Director of Photography: Judy L. Hasday
Senior Production Editor: LeeAnne Gelletly
Publishing Coordinator: James McAvoy
Cover Designer: Terry Mallon

Front Cover Photo: Photofest
Back Cover Photo: Photofest

The Chelsea House World Wide Web address is
http://www.chelseahouse.com

First Printing

1 3 5 7 9 8 6 4 2

Library of Congress Cataloging-in-Publication Data

Hill, Anne E., 1974–
   Cameron Diaz / Anne E. Hill.
   64 p.  cm. – (Galaxy of superstars)
   Filmography: p. 61
   Includes bibliographical references and index.
   Summary: A biography of the model-turned actress who starred in "The
Mask," "My Best Friend's Wedding," and "There's Something About Mary."
   ISBN 0-7910-5234-6 (hc) — ISBN 0-7910-5334-2 (pbk.)
   1. Diaz, Cameron—Juvenile literature  2. Motion picture actors and actresses—
United States—Biography—Juvenile literature. [1. Diaz, Cameron.  2. Actors and
actresses.  3. Women—Biography.]  I. Title.  II. Series.
   PN2287.D4633H56  1999
   791.43'028'092—dc21
   [b]                                                                99—28594
                                                                          CIP
                                                                          AC

Dedication: *For my mom, who has taught me to believe in myself and have fun. And for my husband, who has nurtured both of these traits in me.*

# CONTENTS

# 1

# THERE'S SOMETHING ABOUT SUCCESS

L abor Day weekend is one of the biggest movie-going weekends of the year. Thousands of people flock to the cool darkness of the theater to munch popcorn and enter the world of their favorite stars. Because it is the last unofficial weekend of the summer movie season, many movie companies wait until early September to release the films that they hope will make the biggest impact at the box office. The many movies released the Friday before Labor Day are usually in stiff competition with one another for the coveted number-one spot.

But something unusual happened that first weekend of September in 1998. The number-one movie at the box office was a film that had been out for seven weeks—an almost unheard of occurrence. But even more surprising was the fact that it had never been number one previously, although it had made a significant amount of money. *There's Something About Mary* was a word-of-mouth movie that had become one of the summer's biggest hits. *People* magazine called it "raunchy, sweet, and funny at the same time, always a winning combo." Both praised

---

*Cameron Diaz does not rely only on her dazzling smile and good looks, as many models-turned-movie stars have done. Instead she has worked hard in a series of films that have challenged her craft and brought her phenomenal success.*

and ridiculed for its brand of over-the-top humor, the film had people talking. And one of their favorite subjects was the film's star, Cameron Diaz.

Although she was not an unfamiliar face in Hollywood, this was Diaz's first leading lady role. Judging from the laughter that rang in the theaters every night, she had won over her audience with her acting ability and comic timing. It was a goal that Cameron had been working on since her first on-screen appearance in 1994's *The Mask*. As a former model, Diaz was constantly proving her abilities to people who did not believe that she had the smarts or the savvy to make it in the movies. Being cast as Mary in *There's Something About Mary* gave her career that big boost it needed to make her hot in Hollywood.

Before *There's Something About Mary* was even released, *Entertainment Weekly* (*EW*) named Diaz their "It Girl of 1998." The reason? Her unwillingness not to be just part of the scenery and rely on her staggering good looks, as so many models-turned-movie stars had done before her, even if it meant humiliating herself. In *There's Something About Mary,* "Diaz bravely endures the sickest, most sidesplitting sight gag since [director] John Waters went mainstream," wrote *EW*. While playing the "perfect woman" in the movie, Cameron made sure that a sense of humor was added to the list of desirable attributes, in addition to beauty and intelligence.

The plot of *There's Something About Mary* revolves around four men and their obsession with the beguiling Mary Jenson. As a high school senior in Rhode Island, Ted Stroehmann, played by Ben Stiller, threw caution to the wind and invited Mary to the senior prom. Although she agreed to be his date, they never made it to the dance that night. Ted suffered a humiliating accident in the Jenson's bathroom. Now, more than 12 years later, Ted still cannot get Mary out of his mind. He wants to reunite, or at least know how she is doing. All he knows is that she moved to Miami, Florida, with her family after graduation.

At the insistence of his best friend, Dom, played by Chris Elliot, Ted hires private detective Pat Healy (Matt Dillon) to track her down. But when Pat does find Mary, he finds himself falling for her. Mary is just as beautiful as she was at 17 and is now a successful doctor who selflessly donates her time to help the handicapped. Healy lies to Ted, telling him that Mary is an overweight mother of four children who has never married. Healy then moves to Miami and pretends to be the man of Mary's dreams. He has learned what she wants in a relationship by having listened in on a conversation between Mary and her girlfriends while working for Ted as a detective.

Despite the less-than-appealing picture Healy painted of his high school sweetheart, Ted decides to go to Florida and see Mary himself. He finds out that Healy lied to him, which only adds to his determination to win back Mary's affection. Added to the mix are Dom and Tucker. Dom was actually Mary's out-of-town boyfriend whom she dumped before the prom, and Tucker is a pizza delivery boy posing as a handicapped architect. Each of the four men wants Mary as his own and will stop at nothing to beat the others.

"Mary has four guys falling in love with her who have no idea how to make a charming entrance into her life," Diaz explained.

In addition to these men fighting among themselves for Mary's affection, there is also a more recent ex-boyfriend with whom they must contend—Green Bay Packers' quarterback Brett Favre. While the NFL player had never previously appeared in a film, he gladly took two days off from his busy schedule to make a cameo appearance as himself.

*There's Something About Mary* is a wild film full of somehow humorous disasters and outrageous, often offensive, antics. "They cross every line in this movie, which is outrageous and totally unique. . . . The thing you learn very quickly with Peter and Bobby is that you can never go too far," Diaz said of the screenwriting and directing duo, Peter and Bobby Farrelly, the two brothers who became best known for *Dumb & Dumber* and *Kingpin*.

When asked about how she felt playing the object of all these men's affection and whether she sees herself in the character, Diaz said, "That's difficult to answer because you always see yourself in your character. But although Mary did seem familiar, I always approached her as a character."

Part of Cameron's approach was to conduct research for her part. Although only 25 years old during the movie's filming, Cameron found it difficult to remember the way she felt and behaved during her high school years. She returned to her old alma mater to try to jolt her memory. She recalled that she was never as popular in high school as the character Mary was in the film. That came later.

The film's creators, however, see more simi-larities between the two. "Cameron is Mary," said co-director Peter Farrelly. "Like Mary, Cameron seems like the ultimate woman. Every guy on the set was crazy about her." Bobby, the other half of the directorial team, agreed. "Her character is supposed to be the most appealing woman in the world. And, everybody likes Cameron. She's beautiful, sweet, fun, and nice. A great personality."

Surprisingly, the film's lead almost went to

*Cameron and Ben Stiller in a scene from* There's Something About Mary. *The film, with its unique, over-the-top humor, became a huge success. And according to co-director Peter Farrelly, Cameron was just like her character Mary— "every guy on the set was crazy about her."*

*Cameron and actress Helena Bonham-Carter pose for* Chicago Sun-Times *film critic Roger Ebert at the 1998 Toronto International Film Festival. In his first review of Cameron's acting, Ebert had said admiringly that she had "a gorgeous face, a wonderful smile, and a gift of comic timing."*

another actress. While the Farrellys wrote the script with Cameron in mind for the part of Mary, they also liked the way Courtney Cox, star of the television show *Friends*, read for the character. They eventually went with their first inclination, even pushing back filming to accommodate Cameron's busy schedule. Everyone, especially Cameron, was happy with their final choice.

Part of her joy in filming came from sharing the screen with then-boyfriend Matt Dillon, who played the sleazy Pat Healy. Because the two live on separate coasts, he in New York, she in Los Angeles, working on the movie gave them the chance to spend more time together.

Dillon, then 34, whose acting credits included *The Outsiders, Drugstore Cowboy,* and *In & Out,* had been in the spotlight longer than Cameron and he gave her some pointers on how to handle her new-found fame. "He's very gracious with fans," Diaz said. "He gives everyone the time he can afford, because everybody wants to shake your hand and people want an autograph."

Another of Cameron's loved ones was also in *There's Something About Mary.* Her father was one of the inmates in the jail scene with Ben Stiller's character. "He had the long black hair with the silver streaks. They were kind enough not to leave him on the editing floor," Cameron joked. Cameron's mom was also offered a part by the Farrellys, who enjoy giving friends and family walk-on parts in their films, but she turned it down.

Everyone was on hand for the film's July 9, 1998, premiere at the Fox Movie Theater in Westwood, California. An elaborate 1980s state fair–themed party was held after the screening, complete with games that mocked the cast and characters, as well as plenty of food and drink. Even before it hit theaters on July 17, everyone at the opening had their suspicions that the film was going to be a great success, and they were right.

Not only was the film a huge money maker, grossing more than $170 million, but Cameron also won the prestigious New York Film Critics Circle Award for Best Actress, beating veteran actresses Meryl Streep and Susan Sarandon. "You're shocked? I'm shocked! This is some sort of joke," Cameron told *InStyle* magazine. But this was no joke. The award sparked rumors

*Cameron accepting the 1998 New York Film Critics Circle Award for Best Actress. Even with her meteoric rise to success, Cameron remains down-to-earth, humble, and gracious.*

of an Oscar nomination for Diaz, but that early morning wake-up call from the Academy never materialized. However, Cameron and the film were nominated for Golden Globes as the Best Actress in a Comedy or Musical and Best Film/Comedy or Musical, respectively. She also took home the Blockbuster Entertainment Award for Favorite Actress in a Comedy.

The buzz surrounding these surprise wins and nominations did not shock critics, many of whom included the film in their compilations of the 10 best films of 1998. "The old saw is a true one: Dying is easy, and comedy is hard," said Tom Rothman, head of Fox productions. "Cameron Diaz gives a very brave performance, and I can tell you from watching her craft it that it's a product of great skill."

Despite all of the attention and the media blitz surrounding the film, Cameron has remained humble, even a little frightened by her new-found success. She has claimed that she never wants her name to precede the title of a movie the way many big stars insist. "Of all the actors I've met," said Peter Farrelly, "Cameron is the one who truly fears fame."

But with the offers rolling in for other starring roles, Diaz will have to remember that this is what she has been waiting for ever since she was an unknown teenager growing up in Long Beach, California.

# 2

# STARTING OUT

L ong Beach is one of America's largest shipping ports. Located south of Los Angeles, the city is a business and tourist community of palm trees and sunny beaches. The town is also the home of the University of California at Long Beach, a prestigious college with 35,000 students. The mix of work, education, and leisurely California fun drew Emilio Diaz, an oil company foreman, and his wife Billie, an import-export broker, to the city where they decided to raise their family. They already had a young daughter named Chimene when Cameron was born on August 30, 1972. It was Cameron's father, Emilio, who thought of her unusual name, which is a Gaelic expression meaning "crooked stream."

Cameron, or Cami, or Cam, as she is often called by friends and family, is a unique blend of nationalities— Cuban American on her father's side, German, English, and Native American on her mother's. The Diaz family lived in a two-story gray stucco house in a middle-class neighborhood full of other hard-working families. From a young age, Cameron realized how lucky she was to come

---

*Cameron is proud of her heritage, which is a blend of many different nationalities, including Cuban-American, German, English, and Native-American. She has always said how lucky she was to come from such a loving family with such a diverse background.*

17

from such a loving family with a diverse background. "I grew up with Cuban food and with the music. I grew up with the hospitality, passion, and warmth of the Latin family. . . . But because I didn't speak Spanish, people would say 'You're not Spanish! . . . You've got blonde hair and blue eyes.'"

Emilio and Billie stressed individuality and acceptance to their two daughters. Their easygoing nature made the two sisters less rebellious growing up. "They rarely said no to me," Diaz told *Parade* magazine, "so if they did, I knew they had a good reason, and I wouldn't go against them."

But their parents' laid-back attitude did not prevent the two sisters from butting heads with each other. "I adore and love her like nobody ever," Cameron now says of her sister. "But we fought like crazy when we were kids. We were maniacal—everybody in the neighborhood knew that when we started fighting, to step back. We were like two Tasmanian devils. I was a total terror to her, and she was patient with me. She took care of me, looked out for me, was the perfect big sister."

At Los Cerritos Elementary School, Cameron was a good student who enjoyed school. She developed a flair for drama when, in the second grade, she dressed as Mae West for Halloween. "She had jewels, a long dress, high heels. She was good. The dress didn't trip her," remembered her teacher Mrs. Simms. After she became famous, Cameron went back to visit her old elementary school and fielded questions from young fans about such varied subjects as how she stays so thin, who she is dating, and what it is like to be a star. Diaz stressed to the students the importance of

*Sitting in a souped up race car, Cameron flashes a smile and gives a big thumbs up. As a child she was a bit of a tomboy who loved baseball and skate-boarding. Later as a teenager she had a preference for heavy-metal music.*

staying in school and studying.

Even when she moved on to middle school, Cameron continued to get above-average grades. But despite the feminine influences of her older sister, she grew to be somewhat of a tomboy. She preferred playing baseball and skateboard-ing with the boys to shopping at the mall with her female friends. As a young teenager she also developed a love for heavy-metal music. Diaz's mother took her to her first concert, to see the band Van Halen, and Cameron admits to seeing every heavy-metal band that came to Long Beach. Cameron describes herself as "the tough kid with the jeans, the concert shirt with the flannel over it, the comb in the back pocket, and the feathered hair."

By the time she entered Long Beach Polytechnic High School in 1986, Cameron was a confident teen. Because she was so thin, classmates nicknamed her "Skeletor" and often teased her, but Cameron just shrugged it off. Her biggest loves were cheerleading and animals. In fact Cameron once wanted to be a zoologist. She had five birds, three dogs, three cats, and two snakes while growing up. Even today, Cameron brings her cats, Little Man and Kitty, with her on location. "I like spending time with my cat[s], relaxing after a hard day on a movie set," she revealed.

At age 16, Cameron's career desires took a turn in an unexpected direction when she was approached by photographer Jeff Dunas at a party in Los Angeles. Jeff was employed by the Elite agency, one of the largest modeling agencies in the world. He gave Diaz his card and asked her to consider doing a photo shoot. At first, she was skeptical of his intentions. At 5' 9" with piercing blue eyes and silky blond hair, Cameron had heard many lines before from young men who hoped to get to know her. But when she and her father visited the Elite offices they learned the offer from Jeff was for real. "She had a sparkle," Dunas recalled of his famous discovery.

Her parents made sure that Cameron understood her chance at a modeling career was dependent upon finishing high school. Before she graduated, however, her parents allowed her to do her first modeling assignment: an advertisement for *Teen* magazine that paid her $125. "I didn't tell anybody for a really long time," Cameron recalled. "I was kind of weird about it because I went to school with a girl who was a model. I knew how people would sort of talk about her because she was a model."

When Cameron graduated from high school she signed with the Elite agency and a whole new world opened up for her. She was excited about traveling around the world but sad to leave her family and friends. Her mother gave her a gift before she embarked on her new career, a long silver hairpin that could also double as a weapon if she were confronted by an attacker. "Moms are like that," commented Diaz. Cameron traveled to Japan where she made the rounds of agents and showed her portfolio of pictures.

Young, impressionable, and eager to please would-be employers, Cameron was persuaded to model nude to expand her portfolio. When the photos were published without Cameron's consent in *Celebrity Sleuth* magazine in 1995, she was "devastated." Many models, such as former Miss America Vanessa Williams, posed nude at the start of their careers only to have the photos come back to haunt them after they became famous. "I thought it was a crummy thing for this photographer to do. He didn't have any right to sell or give those pictures to anybody."

Living on her own, traveling between the United States and Europe, Cameron learned a lot and grew up fast. "Believe me," Diaz told *Celebsite*, "you can get into a lot of trouble being [a teenager] in a foreign country with no adult telling you when to come home." At 17, she suffered alcohol poisoning and nearly

*The glittering lights along a main street in Tokyo, Japan. Cameron's modeling career allowed her to travel all over the world and meet many interesting people including her first serious boyfriend, Carlos De La Torre.*

died when she mixed various kinds of alcohol at a party. Cameron was so ashamed of her actions that she did not admit the incident to her family for several years.

Overall, Cameron's modeling experiences were mostly positive. In the following years, as the job offers started to come in, Cameron's face helped to sell everything from Coca-Cola to cold cream. She appeared on the covers of many magazines including the prestigious *Mademoiselle* and *Seventeen.* "I really loved modeling. I mean think about it," Cameron shared with *Vogue* magazine. "I'm making money. . . . I got to travel all over the world, meet interesting people."

One of these interesting people was video producer Carlos De La Torre, whom Diaz met in Japan in 1990 and dated for five years. The two met on the set of a job where Cameron was modeling and Carlos was coordinating. Their relationship developed quickly and soon the two were inseparable. Soon they were sharing a two-bedroom apartment in West Hollywood. "He's a great guy, we're still friends," Cameron said of her first serious boyfriend. While the two were happy and in love, they vacationed together in Mexico and even thought about getting married. But they eventually parted in 1995. Cameron later attributed the split-up to her relatively young age and her need to find out who she was.

In 1990, despite the fact that Cameron's modeling career and personal life were in an upswing, she still felt as if something were missing. "I knew I wasn't the prettiest girl [modeling]. But I would go in and have a great time with the clients. I made them laugh." With the help of her agent, Robin Levy, Cameron made the decision to try acting.

At 19, armed with her experience in front of the camera modeling and the memories of her high school drama class, Cameron set to work on her second career as an actress. She gave up the security of her lucrative modeling assignments, where she was now earning as much as $2,000 a day. Suddenly she was forced to worry about the rent. However, Cameron's perseverance and charm didn't keep her from worrying too long.

One day, while in Levy's office, Cameron happened to spot the script for *The Mask*. When Cameron read it, she imagined herself in the role of nightclub singer Tina Carlyle. Although the role of Tina was not a very large one, it was pretty heady to imagine herself

*Cameron dances with Jim Carrey in a scene from* The Mask. *The film, which introduced Cameron to audiences nationwide, was an educational and exciting experience for her, even though the stress of filming led to an ulcer for the new celebrity.*

making her acting debut in a big feature film. She thought she could "handle a comedy," and auditioned for the part.

Getting the role in *The Mask* was not easy due to Cameron's inexperience and the fact that she was not physically what the producers had in mind. But that did not stop her from pursuing the part. The producers wanted Tina to be a Jessica Rabbit-type bombshell, very curvy and glamorous. So Cameron invested $36 in a padded bra and wowed the producers with her new, curvaceous figure. "Getting to read for *The Mask* was luck," Cameron confided to *Movieline* magazine. "Earning it was work." "She tried out as a joke," Levy admits. But 12 callbacks later, Diaz was able to have the last laugh and set to work on her first movie set.

Diaz had been so wrapped up in getting the part and the eventual filming of the movie that she developed an ulcer, a sore in the lining of the stomach that is often caused by excessive worrying. She considered the opportunity well worth the pain.

Working on the film was incredibly exciting and educational for Cameron. Starring opposite comedian Jim Carrey was also fun. "About a month into the movie, I said, 'This is kind of a big film, isn't it?'" she remembered. "And they all said, 'Yes, Cameron. Yes it is.'"

But no one knew just how big *The Mask* would be. "I couldn't conceive that it would open on 2,000 screens the same day," Cameron confided. The film grossed over $100 million, ensured Carrey's stardom, and introduced Cameron to movie audiences. Roger Ebert, part of the notoriously tough movie-critic team Siskel and Ebert, said, "Cameron Diaz is a true discovery in the film, a genuine sex bomb with a gorgeous face, a wonderful smile, and a gift of comic timing. This is her first movie role. . . . It will not be her last." Bill Morrison of the *News and Observer* wrote, "*The Mask* introduces Cameron Diaz as the vamp who literally has Stanley's [the Carrey character] eyes popping out and his tongue unspooling like a fire hose. She has a Veronica Lake quality . . . cool, sultry."

What had begun as a whim was suddenly a serious career, and Cameron was totally ready to pursue it.

# 3

# MODEL-TURNED-ACTRESS

**"I** don't know a whole lot about acting right now," Cameron candidly admitted to a reporter at *Interview* magazine in June of 1994. "Acting is something different to everybody. I just know that if you watch an actor or actress getting better and better, I think that's them just understanding themselves better and better."

Despite Cameron's limited knowledge of acting, at only 22 she knew what she wanted from her next project: something with more substance. She also knew that she needed a new agent who specialized in acting. Diaz decided on Nick Styne of International Creative Management (ICM). "I don't want to go straight into leading roles. I have too much to learn," she wisely told Styne and Rick Yorn, a manager at ICM. While Cameron thought she needed acting lessons, professionals advised her that she was a natural.

Even though Cameron had played the seductress, she knew that she did not want to be typecast as the blond bombshell. She considered a role of a woman confined to wheelchair in the film *Hugo Pool* but instead decided on an independent, dark comedy called *The Last Supper*.

---

*After appearing in* The Mask, *Cameron wanted to find a more serious part and avoid being typecast as a blond bombshell. She chose the role of Jude (pictured here)—that of an icy, distant woman—in* The Last Supper. *Cameron found working in a small-budget, independent movie a rewarding experience.*

The film, a feature debut by director Stacy Title, deals with the beliefs of five graduate students of different backgrounds, races, and genders. The plot revolves around their decidedly devious plan to invite narrow-minded conservatives to a dinner and then spike their wine with arsenic, a fatal poison.

With actor Courtney B. Vance and actress Annabeth Gish lined up to portray fellow grad students, and Jason Alexander, Mark Harmon, Ron Perlman, and Charles Durning to play their chosen victims, Cameron welcomed "the opportunity to work with other actors." While she was offered the part of the pretty ingenue named Paulie, Diaz convinced director Title that she should play Jude. Jude was an icy, distant woman with conflicting ideals, but she also had a sense of humanity that her other dinner partners lacked. For the role she wore sweatshirts, jeans, and minimal makeup. While the film mainly played art houses and did not do well at the box office, Cameron saw the filming as a learning experience and the movie as a chance to show her growing range and diversity as an actress.

Her next role, Cameron believed, would also expand her talents. She was set to star in the big-budget picture *Mortal Kombat* but was forced to pull out of filming when she broke her hand while learning karate for the part.

The next decision Diaz made changed her career, if not her life—she turned away from big-budget films, partly because she did not like the roles and partly because she was not a favorite actress of these large studios due to her inexperience. Instead she decided to go the independent, or "indie," film route, continuing to work on smaller budget movies like *The Last Supper.* Many powerful Hollywood actors and actresses work on several big-budget films so that they can then take on a risky, though rewarding, role in a small, low-paying, independent film that has caught their attention. Then there are those actors and actresses who make a living as independent film stars. Some get "discovered" by big movie companies and leave for the larger studios, while others choose to stay with the indies.

While her next film, *Feeling Minnesota,* did not have a major studio bankrolling its production, Diaz was drawn to the challenges of telling her character Freddie's story. Cameron shared her thoughts saying, "I think that definitely your chances of coming across material in independent films—material that is more interesting and more challenging—is more likely than in big studio films. You always have to leave your doors open to independent films so you have that opportunity."

She also got the opportunity to star opposite Keanu Reeves, beating out 70 other actresses for the coveted part. Reeves, who had just starred in the blockbuster *Speed,* was a big box-office star who had opted for an independent film; Cameron was excited to get to work with him. The chance had almost passed her by. "I got the script a long time ago and everybody kept telling me to read it, but I just didn't get around to it because I thought the position was already filled, so at the last minute I read it. I liked it. And I went in and read it for Stephen Baigelman [director]. And then I read with Keanu and Vincent [D'Onofrio] a day later."

Cameron beat out 70 other actresses for the part of Freddie in Feeling Minnesota, *opposite Keanu Reeves. She took the opportunity to work on this independent film to learn from her costars, and continue to improve her acting skills.*

Cameron played Freddie, the woman in the middle of two feuding brothers, a theme that she would repeat in her next project, *She's the One*. When Freddie is discovered stealing from a strip club owner, she is forced to marry the club's accountant Sam (Vincent D'Onofrio) as a payoff to Sam. Freddie instead falls for Sam's estranged brother Jjaks (Keanu Reeves), whom she meets for the first time at the wedding reception. Freddie and Jjaks get involved and the two are then confronted with the challenge of getting out of Minnesota together.

During filming Diaz made a bold move when she dyed the roots of her famous blond tresses black. She did not want to appear glamorous in the part of a stripper with a seedy background and nowhere to run. While this was not written into the script as one of Freddie's traits, Cameron made the character her own, something she would do more often as she expanded her experience as an actress.

The character of Freddie was the exact opposite of Cameron's first role as Tina Carlyle. "Tina was a cartoon character; Freddie is a girl who has nothing. But if Freddie did have everything, if she was a glamorous girl, I'd still play the part, just because I'm going after what interests me about her and the material."

While the film was panned by critics when it was released and its plot labeled forgettable, the experience of making the film was still memorable for Cameron. "Keanu and Vincent taught me a lot about focus and dedication," she told Bob Strauss of the *Los Angeles Daily News*. "They were also very honest with the characters, so I learned that—along with, y'know, acting tips."

*Cameron Diaz and Matt Dillon met while on location in Minnesota. They happened to be working on different movie sets at the time, but staying in the same hotel. It wouldn't be until almost one year later that they would start dating and begin what was to become a loving and romantic relationship.*

Despite the intensity of the filming, and what Diaz called a lack of sleep while on location in Minnesota, she still found time to cook up some homemade pasta and sauce for the cast and crew, endearing herself to them with her down-to-earth, fun attitude. She also made a new friend, actor Matt Dillon.

Cameron and Dillon happened to be staying in the same hotel. At the time, Dillon was working on the movie *Beautiful Girls* with Uma Thurman and Timothy Hutton. Cameron, fresh from a breakup with long-term live-in Carlos De La Torre, was hesitant about any romantic relationship. However, before leaving Minnesota, Cameron and Matt did exchange phone numbers. Although they did keep in touch with one another, it would be almost a year before the two actually started dating.

In the meantime, 1996 would prove to be an exciting year for 23-year-old Cameron. She was set to play the roles of Heather in *She's the One*, Nathalie in *Head Above Water*, Kimmy in *My Best Friend's Wedding*, and Celine in *A Life Less Ordinary*. She was a sought-after star who was now hearing the phrase "model-turned-actress" attached to her name less and less. This was good news to Diaz, who always thought it was silly. "People just assume you don't have the capacity to think," she lamented.

In addition to her growing list of credits and new-found credibility as an actress, Cameron was about to learn she was the recipient of a prestigious award.

# 4

# STAR OF TOMORROW

The National Association of Theater Owners (NATO)/ ShoWest Convention and Awards is the largest annual international convention for the movie business, bringing delegates from over 30 countries to the United States each year. It is considered an honor to win an award there because actors are being judged by the people who show their films to thousands of moviegoers on a daily basis— the theater owners.

In March of 1996 in Las Vegas, Nevada, Cameron won the NATO/ShoWest Award for Female Star of Tomorrow. Although thrilled with the award, Cameron was noticeably nervous in her acceptance speech, where she thanked her family and friends. It was the first tangible recognition of her hard work and flowering talent.

But she hardly had time to catch her breath and enjoy the award before she was back at work filming *She's the One*, a film written by and starring Ed Burns, creator of *The Brothers McMullen*. Like Cameron, Burns was also in his 20s, relatively inexperienced, and open to criticism and input from his cast. Cameron enjoyed working with young

*A glamorous Cameron accepts the 1997 Blockbuster Entertainment Award for Favorite Supporting Actress in a Comedy for her role in* My Best Friend's Wedding. *With the film's success Cameron moved up from a working actress to a movie star.*

and first-time directors, finding that it helped her as well. Cameron commented:

> I love it because I get to learn with them. It's trial and error, and we all go into an experience bouncing off one another. The energy is great. There's a sense of like, 'What will happen next?' It's fun to discover that with somebody for your first time [when it's] their first time as well.

Cameron admired Burns. After reading the draft of his script she agreed to play Heather, an aggressive, Wall Street business woman who gets between two brothers, one whom she was once engaged to marry, the other with whom she is currently having an affair. During filming Cameron approached Burns about softening her character. "I gave suggestions of what I thought would serve the story better," she told the *Los Angeles Daily News* just before the film's release in September 1996. "Heather, who is basically the bad girl, was pretty ruthless in the first draft I read. There was nothing redeeming about her; in the end you didn't care about her—in fact, you just hated her. I thought that was just way over the top, in that if you didn't care about her, you wouldn't care about anyone else. You couldn't understand why these men would be fighting about such an ugly human being."

Burns took Cameron's suggestions about the character to heart. He rewrote her character, adding, changing, and taking out scenes from the film. "I can't thank her enough," Burns later said of Diaz. "This character is much more complex than I had initially scripted. It's a funnier, more honest part and a lot of that is because of Cameron's input."

The result was a terrific performance by Cameron and many very good reviews by the critics. *People* magazine wrote: "Diaz shows she may be a Jean Harlow for the '90s—a tough-talking bombshell who isn't afraid to be the butt of the joke. If you're looking for an MVP (Most Valuable Player), Diaz is the one."

Diaz was being recognized more and more and she was suddenly on every reporter's interview list. What the media most admire about Cameron is how down-to-earth and humble she is, despite being a star. Cameron has a loud, raucous laugh that comes from deep in her stomach and splinters the air, sometimes

*The cast of* She's the One. *From left: Edward Burns, Maxine Bahns, Cameron Diaz, Jennifer Aniston, and Mike McGlone. Thanks to suggestions from Cameron, her character, Heather, was rewritten and became funnier and more appealing.*

*Cameron took the part of Nathalie in* Head Above Water *because she wanted to work with veteran actor Harvey Keitel (pictured here). However she did not enjoy several scenes in which she had to spend many hours going in and out of 50°F water, in take after take.*

scaring the reporters and people who are not ready for the unusual sound. In interviews she dresses casually, with little or no makeup, and fields questions from reporters. Speaking candidly, Cameron talks about Matt Dillon, jokes with reporters about her ability to max out her credit cards while shopping, and discusses her less-than-healthy eating habits. "I'm a salty, greasy girl," she told Patrick Demarchelier of *Harper's Bazaar* magazine. "I give every french fry a fair chance." For Cameron, blessed with a good metabolism and a tall 5' 9" frame, the effects of the french fries never show.

Lucky for Cameron, since her next film, *Head Above Water*, featured her in a tiny bathing suit for much of the film. She portrayed Nathalie, the much-younger wife of the character played by actor Harvey Keitel. Diaz once again played the object of many men's affections and was the only female lead in this film, whose plot involved Nathalie's finding the dead body of an ex-boyfriend.

While Cameron took the role mainly for the opportunity to work with veteran actor Harvey Keitel, she admired her other costars as well and, of course, she had a lot of fun on the set. When asked by Susan Lambert of *Boxoffice Online* how she like working with Harvey Keitel, Cameron swooned, "I loo-ooved Harvey," then continued, "[The film] is very dark. It's rather twisted, which was something we had a lot of fun doing."

One thing that was not enjoyable about the film were the water scenes. The water temperature ranged between only 50 and 60 degrees Fahrenheit, and a shivering Cameron completed take after take. "It's the kind of cold that you don't even know you're cold because you can't feel anything. It goes straight to your bones, right through your muscles."

Her work did not go unnoticed in this independent film, and Cameron received praise for her role. Instead of jumping right into her next big-budget studio film, Cameron took time out to make a cameo in another small independent film called *Keys to Tulsa*, appearing as Trudy. She had become known as an indie girl, but was about to make a sudden career change.

Cameron set to work finding an apartment,

*Cameron and Matt Dillon got together whenever their schedules allowed. Here Cameron scours the flea market for hidden treasures while Matt takes a short break. Even with her movie-star status, Cameron still maintains her practical sensibilities.*

her first on her own since her breakup with Carlos. She had been living out of her suitcase, occasionally staying with friends when she was not traveling from location to location. Now she wanted to establish some roots of her own and decided on the downtown Los Angeles neighborhood of Hancock Park.

While many of her model friends blew their earnings on luxury items, Cameron's middle-class upbringing taught her to save. Although she was now in a position to buy a big house and new furniture, Cameron opted to rent both an apartment and the furniture. Months later, once she could envision how it should look, she slowly started buying her own furniture, scouring neighborhood flea markets to find just the right pieces. The one celebrity indulgence that she allowed herself was a new black Mercedes sedan.

Inside her modest but warm apartment, Cameron enjoyed the company of her two cats, spent time reading her favorite authors—Charles Bukowski and Raymond Carver—and wrote in her three journals. "One for travel, one for home, and one I write in before bed," she explained. "But the last thing I want is other people reading it. What's really fun is reading your journal, like a year later, or even a month, and realizing how much you've changed."

She also concocted a plan for Hollywood survival:

> It's been important for me to be happy, enjoy the work that I'm doing, and work with people that I feel I'm going to get something out of. It's not about money, I know I can make a living. I don't live above my means. . . . I don't want to live in a huge house, I just want to be able to provide for myself and my family the things that are essential.

Another plus to her new L.A. address was the closeness to her family in nearby Long Beach. Even though she had called her mother and father every day while filming, she could now stop in for a conversation and some parental advice. "It's just part of my life; for me, there's no other real way. My mom's my best friend; just because I know actors now and I have other circles to run in doesn't mean that I forget the most important people in my life. My family is very proud, they respect me, and they definitely encourage me." The family also had reason to celebrate. Cameron's older sister, Chimene, who had married while Cam was filming *The Mask*, had just had a little baby girl, and Cameron loved being near her new niece, Chloe.

Unfortunately the other important person in Diaz's life, Matt Dillon, had a home base in New York City, so the two were in the midst of a bicoastal, long-distance relationship. Despite the inconvenience, the relationship was getting serious. Dillon, who was reportedly known for his inability to commit in past relationships, was taken with Cameron. The two were often spotted by the media in a romantic embrace. Still, like any relationship, it required effort. Cameron assured curious reporters:

> It's hard to just pop over for the evening. We have to almost schedule our meetings and just get together when we can. We arrange to meet up in different cities. We talk every day on the phone and we're very involved in each other's lives. It's not a superficial thing. . . . Matt is incredible for me to be with at this moment in my life. He's been an actor for 15 years. He knows what kind of demands the business puts on a person. He's not covetous of my time and that's important for an actress. I love him.

Cameron could not have been happier with her life in the summer of 1996. Her career and love life were in an upswing. And in August, as she turned 24, she appeared on the cover of *Rolling Stone* magazine's "Hot" issue. While her beautiful face had graced countless magazine covers as a model, this was her first solo cover as an actress. Diaz had enjoyed modeling, but acting was her calling. She knew there would be no more career changes—she was in love with acting.

She even compared love and acting in an interview in September 1996: "When you're in love with somebody, you have no control over it, you have to be with that person. With my career, I love what I do, so I'm caught now. I'm doing what makes me happy."

# 5

# BIG-BUDGET FILMS

After Cameron's ulcer from shooting *The Mask* and her broken hand sustained during pre-production for *Mortal Kombat*, big movie companies became slightly wary of her dependability, and she happily made a career out of acting in smaller, independent films. However, by the latter half of 1996, Diaz had proven her abilities and found herself appearing opposite Julia Roberts in the potential blockbuster *My Best Friend's Wedding.*

Cameron was happy for the change and for the chance to work closely with Julia Roberts, who is considered one of the most powerful women in Hollywood. Cameron was also delighted to be in a less physically demanding role. "In my previous roles, I was tied up, I was shot at, I was beaten," Cameron lamented. "If I was driving a car it was because I was being chased. Finally I get to stay clean, I get to wear open-toed shoes, I get to smile through a whole movie because that's my weapon."

Diaz was pleasantly surprised with the big-studio film experience as a whole and happy to have found a worthwhile role. She confided during filming:

*Cameron was pleasantly surprised with her experience in the hit film* My Best Friend's Wedding. *Here, opposite movie superstar Julia Roberts in a scene from this big-budget film, Cameron uses her sweet smile as a weapon to successfully win over Julia and the audience.*

*For her scene in a karaoke bar (here with Dermot Mulroney and Julia Roberts), Cameron was terrified because she did not consider herself a very good singer. In fact, after many takes, her loud laugh "scrambled" the karaoke machine.*

[W]omen's roles are just lacking, period. But there are a lot of very intelligent actresses out there who are gaining more power, which gives them the ability to take something they like and work it into something they love. I think we're going to see a lot more of that. . . . I think certainly the role Julia is playing is a great role and my character is great as well. So I feel happy with the decision of doing this film, even though it's a studio film. I think it's definitely a good role.

As the character Kimmy Wallace, Cameron plays a woman who unknowingly gets between best friends Julianne Potter (Roberts) and Michael O'Neal, played by Dermot Mulroney. Julianne and Michael, who met and dated briefly in college, made a pact that if they had not married by age 28 they would marry each other. Nine years later, and weeks before their 28th birthdays, Michael calls Julianne with the news that he is engaged and getting married to Kimmy that weekend. Suddenly, Julianne realizes that she, not Kimmy, is the right woman for Michael. She goes to the wedding with sabotage on her mind and plans to get Michael back.

Problems ensue from the start when Kimmy asks Julianne to be her maid of honor. Having heard so much about Michael's best friend, Kimmy is enamored of Julianne. Despite her incredible wealth, beauty, and the fact that she has the man they both love, Kimmy is very sweet to Julianne. Julianne hates herself for despising the unaffected and unassuming Kimmy but is still determined to ruin the wedding. As Julianne explains to her friend George in the film, "What I mean when I say she's annoyingly perfect is that there is nothing annoying about her perfection. It is vulnerable and endearing. . . . If I didn't have to hate her, I'd adore her."

During filming in Chicago the cast stayed in one hotel and spent countless hours together. They quickly bonded, making Cameron slightly less uncomfortable with a difficult scene in which her character is forced to sing at a karaoke bar, a bar with a machine that has pre-recorded music that lets people sing along with their favorite tunes. In the film's karaoke scene, Julianne, hoping to embarrass Kimmy in front of Michael, has her plans backfire. Although Kimmy's performance begins tentatively out-of-tune, it ends with her happily belting out the song while the entire bar cheers along. While many actors and actresses can sing as well as act, Cameron is not one of these harmonic few. "I was terrified, I was hoping that I could be as consistently horrible as possible so the karaoke scene could end. There were a few times where I guess I hit a few notes and P. J. Hogan, the director, would say, 'That sounded good Cameron. Now change it,'" she joked. After days of shooting Cameron actually broke the karaoke machine. "Somehow I'd picked the hardest song ["I Just Don't Know What To Do With Myself"] to sing, thinking it was easy," laughed Cameron. "I have this loud, braying laugh that scrambled the karaoke screen. They had to bring in a technician to fix it."

Despite the many obstacles the characters Kimmy and Michael encounter, they do make it down the aisle. Shooting the wedding was a production in and of itself. "Movie weddings are tricky," director Hogan said. "They are judged harshly. Some people go primarily to see the wedding, and some rate the film by the ceremony. Everyone has a concept of a wedding. So it is important to try to be inventive. A lot of work should go into staging a movie wedding, because it is a ritual guaranteed to produce a certain amount of madness."

Filmed at the Fourth Presbyterian Church on Michigan Avenue, the ceremony featured 7,000 white Tenaki roses, which were flown in from Ecuador, as well as a wedding dress made especially for Cameron. Made of a white silk-satin, the dress featured hand-beaded Austrian crystals, a silk tulle veil, and a 14' train. "It was very heavy, nearly thirty pounds of tulle," explained Cameron. "It took about five people to transport me from one place to the next when wearing it."

With its star-studded cast, good story line, and fun Burt Bachrach tune-filled sound-track, *My Best Friend's Wedding* was destined to be a hit. Released in June 1997, it grossed $127 million. Riding on the film's success, Cameron went from a working actress to a movie star, and won the Blockbuster Entertainment Award for Favorite Supporting Actress in a Comedy.

Even before the film's release, she was on to her next project. While she was filming *My Best Friend's Wedding,* Cameron read the script of *A Life Less Ordinary.* She knew that it would be her next movie and convinced director Danny Boyle of her talents. "I wanted somebody who was almost mythically American," Boyle said. "And somebody who would respond well to Ewan [McGregor] and his sense of humor. . . . As soon as she walked in the room I knew she was right. She was unlike any of the other actresses I had met; very natural, very fun-loving and with a great sense of humor."

Diaz landed the role opposite British star Ewan McGregor, who played the part of Robert. They spent the fall of 1996 filming the dark comedy. "We laughed for two months solid. Ewan is a remarkable talent. Everything he does for the camera is so truthful and believable," Cameron raved of her costar. "I play Celine Naville. She's a very spoilt, very cynical, very rich girl, who loathes her cold-hearted father, Robert's boss, and will do almost anything to irritate and pain him," Cameron explained. "She gets herself kidnapped by Robert, this poor, helpless guy who doesn't know what he's got himself into. He takes her, thinking that he's in control of the situation, when really she's the one who's in control."

*Playing Celine, the manipulative, spoiled rich girl opposite British actor Ewan McGregor (pictured here) in the dark comedy A Life Less Ordinary, Cameron displays her skills at character development, which not only gave her valuable experience but also many favorable reviews.*

The film bombed, but Cameron expressed her appreciation by saying that working with the cast and crew of *A Life Less Ordinary* was "the best filmmaking experience . . . yet."

She also received good reviews for playing Celine. *Premiere* magazine wrote, "Diaz has a studied coldness that can take a long time to thaw out, and this is utilized brilliantly, even when she's gagged and bound to a chair, she's still the most intimidating person on screen."

Upon the film's completion, Cameron decided to take a long, much-needed break. But she first made another cameo appearance in an indie film entitled *Fear and Loathing in Las Vegas*, where she played a television reporter. Diaz had two projects lined up for the end of

1997—*Very Bad Things* and *There's Something About Mary.*

She found 1996 to be an extremely rewarding and exhausting year. "For the first time in my life, I took time off. I sat around for 10 months, and I thought that was the hugest blessing anybody could ever have. I feel really fortunate to have a job that allows me to do that." She spent as much time as possible with her family and Matt and enjoyed waking up in the same place every day.

> I didn't know what it was like to be on my own, without having a call time the next morning, without knowing what was going to happen the next day. . . . [A]lso when you do a part, you take on some of the identity of the character. I wanted to know what it was like to not have those influences, and so I'd wake up and think 'What would Cameron do? Where would Cameron go?'

Cameron enjoyed the time off after three years of back-to-back movie making. One thing she did not do during her break was follow the media blitz surrounding her. She revealed to actor Ben Stiller that she does not even own a television set. Ben Stiller admiringly confessed in an article for *Jane* magazine, "Any woman who is in the world of entertainment and pop culture, is acting in movies, is in one of the most competitive environments in the world and doesn't even care to have a television on which to keep score, is already a Zen master, as far as I'm concerned."

After working with the actress and interviewing her, Ben Stiller has joined the long list of people who have fallen for Cameron Diaz and her many charms.

# 6

# CAMERON'S BIG
# ADVENTURE

Only a small, elite group of actors can pick and choose their own roles from many scripts and request a larger salary for every role they take because they have proved that their movies are repeated blockbusters. This "A-List," as it is called, includes actors such as Tom Cruise, Tom Hanks, Jim Carrey, and Arnold Schwarzenegger. While fewer females are included, Julia Roberts, Meg Ryan, and Sandra Bullock are all powerful Hollywood actresses who have been linked to the famous A-List. Suddenly, in 1998, Cameron's name was also among the list of stars expected to become Hollywood superstars.

In addition to her acting abilities and high-profile relationship with Dillon, Cameron was also considered to embody a unique sense of style. Designers wanted to court her into wearing their latest creations. Cameron's fashion sense at parties and premieres was featured on the pages of many fashion and entertainment magazines, and her hair, makeup, and clothing styles were emulated by women everywhere.

The recognition and adoration were strange for her at

*Cameron shows her sense of style at the 1999 New York Film Critics Circle Awards. There she won the Best Actress award for her role in* There's Something About Mary. *Cameron's wonderful fashion sense has kept her on the pages of entertainment and fashion magazines nationwide.*

*While working on* There's Something About Mary, *Cameron and her costar Matt Dillon were a couple in real life. Cameron later said that laughing and having fun on the set brought them even closer together.*

first. "[P]eople went from looking at me and going 'Where do I know you from? What school did you go to?' to, 'Hey, you're Cameron Diaz!' Within three days, all of a sudden, people knew my name."

People wanted to know much more about the blond-haired, blue-eyed beauty. She was the subject of discussions, interviews, and speculation. Many interviewers were amazed to hear that Cameron was actually Hispanic, thinking possibly the name Diaz was created for theatrical purposes. "I think there are enough stereotypes in this industry—and in society in general," Cameron answered in an interview for the website *E!Online* when questioned about her background. "My Latin roots are very strong. . . . Being Latin is part of who I am—and I bring that part to every role."

By October of 1997, Cameron was ready for more roles. She was set to play the lead in *There's Something About Mary*, with Matt Dillon in a costarring role, and was also preparing to play yet another bride in a dark comedy called *Very Bad Things*. So it was back to work, which was made easier by being with Dillon every day.

The cast and crew of *Mary* were amazed at how Diaz and Dillon separated their professional and personal lives. They were always in character in front of the camera, and they behaved as true colleagues when discussing a scene. But during breaks and on the weekends they were a couple very much in love. "Matt would come over and rub her shoulders . . . if it had been a long day," costar Lin Shaye told *People* magazine. "I would notice them sitting on a bench together, or stretching out with her head on his chest. They were affectionate in a really gentle way."

Even before the film's release in July 1998, the two were getting requests for interviews as a couple. They were featured on the cover of *Harper's Bazaar* with the headline "The Real-Life Romance of Cameron Diaz & Matt Dillon." In the interview Dillon admitted, "I was on the fence about playing Healy. But Cameron said, 'Honey, you know how you're always lying to me? You'd be really good at this. You're such a pathological liar.'" The two then broke into laughter.

"We don't try to hide anything," Cameron said in another interview with *E!Online*. "We are who we are. We're a couple. We're affectionate in a way that's comfortable for us in public. We try to live our lives the way we would if we were not famous."

Besides the personal pluses to taking the role, Dillon found that playing Healy also had professional benefits. His 20-year-old career had needed a boost. Dillon had started acting at just 14 and had known fame early as a teen and young adult in films such as *The Outsiders* and *The Flamingo Kid*. Like Cameron he had spent a lot of time making independent films in the '90s. He also enjoyed a close relationship with his family. While the two had always wanted to act together in a film, they had imagined they would collaborate on a more romantic picture. But *There's Something About Mary* struck a nerve and made them laugh. Laughing and having fun, Cameron believes, are essential in life. "Making movies, it's fun, it's fun, *it's fun*," she gushed to *Premiere* magazine.

Fun was exactly what Diaz had when she joined the cast of *Saturday Night Live* to host their season premiere in September 1998. In her opening monologue Diaz picked on people in the audience, giving them a glimpse of her playing a tough girl, nothing like the sweet Mary Jenson they had all loved on the big screen. She then joined regular cast members in some comedic skits where even more of her tremendous sense of humor shone through. Cam played everything from a ditzy talk show host on a parody of Barbara Walters's *The View*, to one of Shakespeare's famous "three witches," accidentally mixing up a batch of smelly brew.

Her next screen role also lived up to her rule of having fun. The film *Very Bad Things* marked Cameron's third stint as a bride. Writer/director Peter Berg described her character, Laura, as "a young Martha Stewart with a bad case of rabies." The film, an ensemble piece, starring Christian Slater, Jon Favreau, and Daniel Stern, was shot in only 35 days,

and Cameron's scenes took just three weeks to film.

The movie tells the story of a Las Vegas bachelor party turned deadly when the drunken and drugged revellers accidentally kill the stripper called in for the occasion. Cameron's character is so obsessed with her plans that when she learns of the killing, she only scolds her fiancé for nearly ruining the wedding. Released during the Thanksgiving weekend of 1998, the film's all-star cast could not lure people to the theaters, however, and *Very Bad Things* was one of the most critically and financially disappointing films of the year.

*In 1998 Cameron continued to have fun by appearing on* Saturday Night Live *with Dan Aykroyd (on her left) and Steve Martin (on her right). In that sketch the two men played the original "wild and crazy guys."*

Yet the lack of success of the film could not take the shine off Cameron Diaz's year. She was named one of *Entertainment Weekly*'s Rising Hollywood Powers, and she reportedly will make $10 million for her work in the upcoming film *Success* with Meryl Streep. She has completed *Being John Malkovich* and the upcoming Oliver Stone film, *Any Given Sunday,* in which she plays the manager of a pro football team. In May 1999 she began filming the Fine Line drama *Invisible Circus* in Paris, in which she appears in a series of flashbacks as a woman who committed suicide.

Although the filming took place in Paris, one of the most romantic cities in the world, Matt Dillon did not visit her there. Despite rumors that Dillon had been spotted shopping for engagement rings, the two broke off their almost three-year relationship in September 1998. Reportedly they no longer wanted to live apart but could not decide whether to live in New York or Los Angeles.

While the breakup was hard on Cameron, she had many projects to keep her busy and showed no signs of slowing down. In the future, she said, she would focus on more reality-based plots. Just as she chose not to go the bombshell route after *The Mask*, Diaz decided not to be strictly a comic actress after the release of *There's Something About Mary.*

She wants her career, like her life, to be varied and full of different experiences. "Acting allows me to tell a lot of stories, you know start at the beginning, finish at the end and tell everything in between."

Even though Cameron is now considered an actress and not a model, she is still noted for her incredible beauty. She was named one of *People* magazine's "50 Most Beautiful People" of 1998. The actress who never wanted to rely on her looks has accomplished the task, but her looks still cannot go unnoticed by both castmates and audiences everywhere. Her costumer Leesa Evans said, "[Cameron] allows who she is to come through without fear. . . . She doesn't get too caught up in over-analyzing what beauty is." Costar Jim Carrey raved, "Cami is an extremely cool human, despite having what normally can be character-crippling good looks."

Cameron would rather talk about acting. When questioned about her looks, she credits her mother for making her comfortable with her appearance. "I don't always love my body," she admitted. "But I was fortunate that I grew up with my mom, who I never heard once complain about her body. Anything that she was unhappy with, she would say, 'This is where I am right now, and hopefully later I'll do the things that I need to do.'" However, most people would argue that Cameron does not need to do anything to better herself.

Cameron's tremendous talent has ignited the screen and her star continues to burn bright. She simply continues to be herself and live life to the fullest. As director Peter Berg said, Cameron Diaz is "trying to live an adventure and not have it swallow her up." So far, Cami has more than succeeded and can look forward to many more on-screen and off-screen adventures.

# CHRONOLOGY

| | |
|---|---|
| 1972 | Cameron Diaz born on August 30 in Long Beach, California. |
| 1986 | Enters Long Beach Polytechnic High School. |
| 1988 | Discovered by photographer Jeff Dunas of Elite Modeling Agency. |
| 1989 | Signs contract with Elite and travels to Europe and Japan to model. |
| 1990 | Meets and begins dating Carlos De La Torre. |
| 1993 | Auditions for her first movie role in *The Mask* and gets the part after 12 readings. |
| 1994 | *The Mask* is released. |
| 1995 | Stars in *The Last Supper*; ends relationship with Carlos; shoots *Feeling Minnesota*; meets Matt Dillon. |
| 1996 | *She's the One*, *Feeling Minnesota*, and *Head Above Water* released; wins ShoWest Female Star of Tomorrow Award. |
| 1997 | Costars with Julia Roberts in *My Best Friend's Wedding*; *A Life Less Ordinary* released. |
| 1998 | Receives Blockbuster Entertainment Favorite Supporting Actress Award for *My Best Friend's Wedding*; *There's Something About Mary* and *Very Bad Things* released; relationship with Matt Dillon ends; wins New York Film Critics Circle Award for Best Actress for *Mary*; nominated for Golden Globe Award for Best Actress in a Comedy or Musical for *Mary*. |
| 1999 | *Being John Malkovich* and *On Any Given Sunday* scheduled for release; named to *Premiere* magazine's list of 100 Most Powerful People in Hollywood; wins Blockbuster Entertainment Favorite Actress in a Comedy Award for *There's Something About Mary*; in talks to appear in movie version of "Charlie's Angels" with Drew Barrymore. |
| 2000 | *Success*, costarring Meryl Streep, scheduled for release. |

# FILMOGRAPHY

1994    *The Mask*

1995    *The Last Supper*

1996    *She's the One*
        *Feeling Minnesota*
        *Head Above Water*

1997    *Keys to Tulsa*
        *My Best Friend's Wedding*
        *A Life Less Ordinary*

1998    *Fear and Loathing in Las Vegas*
        *There's Something About Mary*
        *Very Bad Things*

1999    *Being John Malkovich*
        *On Any Given Sunday*

2000    *Success*

# AWARDS

1996    ShoWest Female Star of Tomorrow Award

▸ 1998   Blockbuster Entertainment Favorite Supporting Actress Award
        for *My Best Friend's Wedding*; New York Film Critics Circle Best
        Actress Award for *There's Something About Mary*

1999    Blockbuster Entertainment Favorite Actress in a Comedy Award
        for *There's Something About Mary*

# FURTHER READING

Bart, Peter. *The Gross: The Hits, The Flops—The Summer that Ate Hollywood.*
New York: St. Martin's Press, 1999.

Demarchilier, Patrick. "A Fine Romance." *Harper's Bazaar*, August 1998.

———. "Splashing Out." *Harper's Bazaar*, July 1996.

Gliatto, Tom. "Unmasked: Cameron Diaz is the beauty who tames Jim
Carrey's party beast." *People,* August 22, 1994.

Hofler, Robert. "The Year of Living Famously." *Premiere*, December 1998.

Lambert, Susan. "Candid Cameron." *Boxoffice Online*, September 1996.

Oliver, Lauren. "Lights, Cameron, Action!" *Interview*, August 1994.

Rosen, David. *Off Hollywood: The Making and Marketing of Independent
Films.* Grove Press, 1990.

Schneider, Karen S. "There's Something About Cameron." *People*,
September 8, 1998.

Seiler, Andy. "'Mary's nominations start something." *USA Today*, December
21, 1998.

Stiller, Ben. "Mutual Admiration in the Afternoon." *Jane*, Volume 2, Number
7, September 1998.

Strauss, Bob. "Cameron Diaz Talks about Role Choices." *Los Angeles Daily
News*, September 9, 1996.

# ABOUT THE AUTHOR

ANNE E. HILL holds a B.A. in English from Franklin and Marshall College, where she was a member of Phi Beta Kappa and wrote for the *Franklin and Marshall College* magazine. A freelance writer, she has also written the Chelsea House titles *Denzel Washington*, which was named to the list of "Best Books for the Teenage" by the New York Public Library; *Ekaterina Gordeeva*; and *Female Firsts in Their Fields: Broadcasting & Journalism*. Mrs. Hill is also a writer for the All-Stars Teen Hotline, run by the Concert Connection. She lives in Wayne, Pennsylvania, with her husband, George. *My Best Friend's Wedding* and *She's the One* are her favorite Cameron Diaz films.

---

# INDEX

64